MW00437890

To a dear friend

The Heart of a *Friend*

A N D R E W S   A N D   McM E E L

A UNIVERSAL PRESS SYNDICATE COMPANY

K A N S A S   C I T Y

ISBN: 0-8362-4247-5
Library of Congress Catalog Card Number: 94-73314

First U.S. edition

1 3 5 7 9 10 8 6 4 2

Edited by Linda Sunshine
Designed by Pat Tan

Produced by Smallwood and Stewart, Inc., New York City

Notice: Every effort has been made to locate the copyright owners of the material used in the book. Please let us know if an error has been made, and we will make any necessary changes in subsequent printings.

Credits and copyright notices appear on pages 94–95

*M*ore than 2,000 years ago, the Roman poet Catullus wrote:

Friendship is here, my heart

Richer than love or passion

In these two lines, he expressed one of the most enduring aspects of friendship, for even when love and passion fade, it is friendship that sustains us. Indeed, friendship is the foundation for almost every relationship in our lives, from family members to casual acquaintances. It is no wonder, then, that poets, novelists, playwrights, and writers of nonfiction throughout the ages have pondered the concept of friendship.

The subject is as elusive as love, perhaps more so, for the boundaries of friendship are uncharted. In his novel *Crossing to Safety*, Wallace Stegner writes about four characters who are ". . . drawn together, braided and plaited into a friendship." He describes both the rewards and complications of this emotional entanglement and of all great friendships: "It is a relationship that has no formal shape, there are no rules or obligations or bonds as in marriage or the family, it is held together by neither law nor property nor blood, there is no glue in it but mutual liking. It is therefore rare."

Rare indeed, for friends are the people we choose to bring into our lives, and we either keep them close or allow them to slip away. It has often been said that a friend is like a mirror through which we see ourselves reflected. Thus, our friends define who we are and what we need from each other.

The idea for this book is rooted in the importance of friendship. Here we celebrate the relationships that define our lives from earliest childhood through old age with words from such diverse and gifted writers as Elizabeth Barrett Browning, E. B. White, Ralph Waldo Emerson, Dorothy Parker, Henry Wadsworth Longfellow, Gloria Naylor, Henry Brooke Adams, Phyllis Theroux, John Keats, Walt Whitman, and many others. On every page, we acknowledge and honor the comfort and connection that only a friend can bestow and offer thanks for that loving person who we are lucky enough to call "friend."

LINDA SUNSHINE

And the song,

from beginning to end,

I found in the heart of a friend.

HENRY WADSWORTH LONGFELLOW
The Arrow and the Song

The days may come,

The days may go,

*B*ut still the hands of memory weave

*T*he blissful dreams of long ago.

GEORGE COOPER
Sweet Genevieve

ut she gave me her photograph,
and printed "Ever Thine"
Across the back ~ in blue-and-red ~
That old sweetheart of mine!

JAMES WHITCOMB RILEY
An Old Sweetheart of Mine

One day in the middle of March
I met Phyllis Green in the doorway of MacFarland's
Candy Store. Although Phyllis and I had gone to the same school
for over a year, we had never approached each other. . . . Phyllis had
skinny legs and big feet, and so did I. There was usually a hole in the back
of one of her socks, and the socks always rode down in her large, down-
at-the-heels shoes. . . . Phyllis was carefree, happy; and I ~ I was already
like an unhappy mouse. She was my best friend for a while.

DELORIS HARRISON
A Friend for a Season

Little deeds of kindness,

Little words of love,

Make our earth an Eden,

Like the heaven above.

ANONYMOUS

t was not considered as being formally received into the school, however, until J. Steerforth arrived. Before this boy, who was reputed to be a great scholar, and was very good-looking, and at least half a dozen years my senior, I was carried as

before a magistrate. He inquired, under a shed in the

playground, into the particulars of my punishment,

and was pleased to express his opinion that it was

"a jolly shame": for which I became bound to him

ever afterwards.

CHARLES DICKENS
David Copperfield

riendship is the comfort, the inexpressible comfort of feeling safe with a person, having neither to weigh thoughts nor measure words, but pouring all right out just as they are, chaff and grain together, certain that a faithful hand will take and sift them, keep what is worth keeping, and with a breath of comfort, blow the rest away.

GEORGE ELIOT

These houses made the most of their seaward view, and there was a gayety and determined floweriness in their bits of garden ground; the small-paned high windows in the peaks of their steep gables were like knowing eyes that watched the harbor and the far sea-line beyond, or looked northward all along the shore and its background of spruces and balsam firs. When one really knows a village like this and its surroundings, it is like becoming acquainted with a single person. The process of falling in love at first sight is as final as it is swift in such a case, but the growth of true friendship may be a lifelong affair.

SARAH ORNE JEWETT
The Country of the Pointed Firs

ANNABEL and MIDGE had been best friends almost from the day that Midge had found a job as stenographer with the firm that employed Annabel. By now, Annabel, two years longer in the stenographic department, had worked up to the wages of eighteen dollars and fifty cents a week; Midge was still at sixteen dollars. Each girl lived at home with her family and paid half her salary to its support.

The girls sat side by side at their desks, they lunched together every noon, together they set out for home at the end of the day's work. Many of their evenings and most of their Sundays were passed in each other's company. Often they were joined by two young men, but there was no steadiness to any such quartet; the two young men would give place, unlamented, to two other young men, and lament would have been inappropriate, really, since the newcomers were scarcely distinguishable from their predecessors. Invariably the girls spent the fine idle hours of their hot-weather Saturday afternoons together. Constant use had not worn ragged the fabric of their friendship.

They looked alike, though the resemblance did not lie in their features. It was in the shape of their bodies, their movements, their style, and their adornments. Annabel and Midge did, and completely, all that young office workers are besought not to do. They painted their lips and their nails, they darkened their lashes and lightened their hair, and scent seemed to shimmer from them. They wore thin, bright dresses, tight over their breasts and high on their legs, and tilted slippers, fancifully strapped. They looked conspicuous and cheap and charming.

DOROTHY PARKER
The Standard of Living

When I entered school and became part of society, I realized that the important thing was to attach myself to the most powerful armada in the bay, become part of a fleet of little girls who, by virtue of our collective power, would cut through the waters without fear. In order to make the center hold, I had to be in the center of things. Friends would protect me.

PHYLLIS THEROUX
California and Other States of Grace

*H*ere she had no choice but to be herself. The carefully erected decoys she was constantly shuffling and changing to fit the situation were of no use here. Etta and Mattie went way back, a singular term that

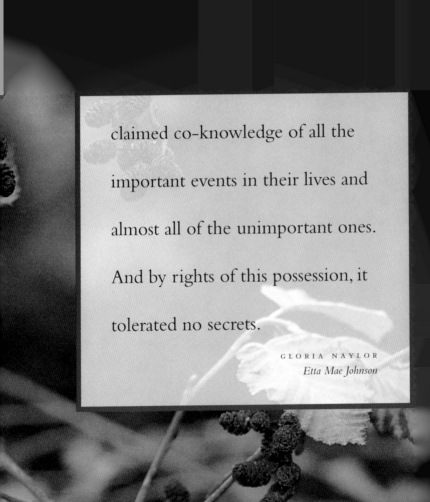

claimed co-knowledge of all the

important events in their lives and

almost all of the unimportant ones.

And by rights of this possession, it

tolerated no secrets.

GLORIA NAYLOR
Etta Mae Johnson

Happiness

is made to be shared.

FRENCH PROVERB

To John Hamilton Reynolds

22 November 1817

My Dear Reynolds,

Whenever I am separated from you and not engaged in a
continued Poem ~ every Letter shall bring you a lyric ~
but I am too anxious for you to enjoy the whole, to send
you a particle. One of the three Books I have with me is
Shakespeare's Poems: I ne'er found so many beauties
in the Sonnets ~ they seem to be full of fine things
said unintentionally ~ in the intensity of working out
conceits. Is this to be borne? Hark ye! . . .

I rest
Your affectionate friend
John Keats

*B*esides ourselves, the car carried the
fragrance of wilted and exhausted
flowers, and the combined weight of
a little too much enjoyment. . . .

COLETTE
Flowers and Fruit

To me, fair friend, you never can be old.

For as you were when first your eye I eyed,

Such seems your beauty still.

WILLIAM SHAKESPEARE
Sonnet 104

*I*t was such a joy to see thee. I wish I could tell

how much thee is to my life. I always turn to thee

as a sort of rest and often just think about thy face

when I get troubled. I am not very good at saying

all I feel, but deep down I do feel it all so much.

LADY HENRY SOMERSET
Philadelphia Quaker

I awoke this morning with devout thanksgiving for my friends, the old and the new. Shall I not call God, the Beautiful, who daily showeth himself so to me in his gifts? I chide

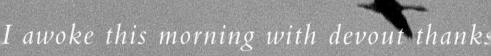

I awoke this morning with devout thanks

society, I embrace solitude, and yet I am not so ungrateful as not to see the wise, the lovely, and the noble-minded, as from time to time they pass my gate.

RALPH WALDO EMERSON
Friendship

iving for my friends, the old and the new

he least flower, with a brimming cup,

And share

may stand.

its dew-drop with another near.

ELIZABETH BARRETT BROWNING

If one could be friendly with
women, what a pleasure ~
the relationship so secret
and private compared with
relationships with men.

VIRGINIA WOOLF
A Writer's Diary

I dream'd in a dream I saw a city invincible to the attacks

   of the whole of the rest of the earth,

I dream'd that was the new city of Friends,

Nothing was greater there than the quality of robust love,

   it led the rest,

It was seen every hour in the actions of the men of that city,

And in all their looks and words.

WALT WHITMAN

The friend who understands

ROMAIN ROLLAND
Journey Within

you,

creates you.

There is nothing we like to see so much as the gleam of pleasure in a person's eye when he feels that we have sympathized with him, understood him, interested ourself in his welfare. At these moments something fine and spiritual passes between two friends. These moments are the moments worth living.

DON MARQUIS
Prefaces

Bewick del

I praise the Frenchman, his remark was shrewd ~

How sweet, how passing sweet, is solitude!

But grant me still a friend in my retreat

Whom I may whisper ~ solitude is sweet!

WILLIAM COWPER
Retirement

Am I not still a lonely man, as far as ever from forming part of the social order? This, of which I once was scornfully proud, seems to be now, if not a calamity, something I would not choose if life were to live again.

GEORGE GISSING
The Private Papers of Henry Ryecroft

I think, from some brief experience of the thing, that as friendships grow old, they seem to depend less on actual contacts and messages in order to maintain their soundness; the growth has got into the wood of the tree, and is there; and yet I am also quite sure that no friendship yields its true pleasure and nobility of nature without frequent communication, sympathy and service.

GEORGE E. WOODBERRY

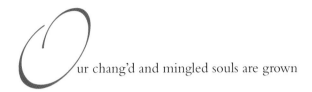Our chang'd and mingled souls are grown

To such acquaintance now,

That if each would resume their own,

Alas! We know not how.

KATHERINE PHILIPS
To Mrs. M. A. at Parting

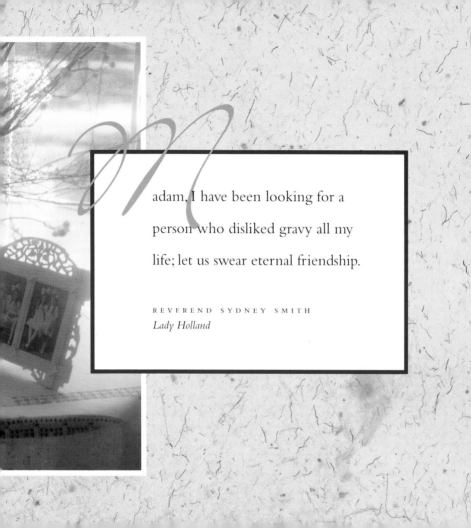

adam, I have been looking for a person who disliked gravy all my life; let us swear eternal friendship.

REVEREND SYDNEY SMITH
Lady Holland

$\mathcal{W}$herever you are it is
your own friends who
make your world.

WILLIAM JAMES
Ralph Barton Perry

Flowers are lovely; love is flower-like;

Friendship is a sheltering tree.

SAMUEL TAYLOR COLERIDGE
Youth and Age

Laughter

can be

more satisfying than honor;

more precious than money;

more heart-cleansing than prayer.

HARRIET ROCHLIN

Fate chooses our relatives,

we choose our friends.

JACQUES DELILLE

I have always felt that the great high privilege, relief and comfort of friendship was that one had to explain nothing.

KATHERINE MANSFIELD

ome of Wilbur's friends in the barn worried for fear all this attention would go to his head and make him stuck up. But it never did. Wilbur was modest; fame did not spoil him. He still worried some about the future, as he could hardly believe that a mere spider would be able to save his life. Sometimes at night he would have a bad dream. He would dream that men were coming to get him with knives and guns. But that was only a dream. In the daytime, Wilbur usually felt happy and confident. No pig ever had truer friends, and he realized that friendship is one of the most satisfying things in the world.

E. B. WHITE
Charlotte's Web

A faithful friend

is the medicine of life.

ECCLESIASTICUS 6:16

he friendships which last are those wherein each friend respects the other's dignity to the point of not really wanting anything from him.

CYRIL CONNOLLY
The Unquiet Grave

Things like sticking to

old friends have really

got bigger to me than

anything else.

SHERWOOD ANDERSON

Love is only

Friends are

GELETT BURGESS

chatter,

all that matter.

No medicine is more valuable, none more efficacious, none better suited to the cure of all our temporal ills than a friend, to whom we may turn for consolation in time of trouble, and with whom we may share our happiness in time of joy.

SAINT AILRED OF RIEVAULX
Christian Friendship

e cherish our friends

but for ours to amuse them.

EVELYN WAUGH

not for their ability to amuse us,

For mem'ry has painted this
        perfect day
With colors that never fade,
And we find, at the end of
        a perfect day,
The soul of a friend we've
        made.

CARRIE JACOBS BOND
A Perfect Bond

One friend in a lifetime is much; two

Friendship needs a certain parallelism of life, a

HENRY BROOKE ADAMS
The Education of Henry Adams

are many; three are hardly possible.

community of thought, a rivalry of aim.

ACKNOWLEDGMENTS

Excerpt from *A Friend for a Season* by Deloris Harrison, copyright © 1972 by Deloris Harrison, reprinted by permission of Harold Ober Associates Incorporated.

Excerpt from "Etta Mae Johnson," from *The Women of Brewster Place* by Gloria Naylor. Copyright © 1980, 1982 by Gloria Naylor. Used by permission of Viking Penguin, a division of Penguin Books USA Inc.

Excerpt from "The Standard of Living," copyright 1941 by Dorothy Parker, renewed © 1969 by Lillian Hellman, from *The Portable Dorothy Parker* by Dorothy Parker, Introduction by Brendan Gill. Used by permission of Viking Penguin, a division of Penguin Books USA Inc.

Excerpt from *California and Other States of Grace* by Phyllis Theroux, copyright © 1980 by Phyllis Theroux, reprinted by permission of William Morrow and Company, Inc.

Excerpt from *Charlotte's Web* by E. B. White, copyright 1952 by E. B. White, renewed © 1980 by E. B. White, reprinted by permission of HarperCollinsPublishers.

Other attributions as follows: Sherwood Anderson from the *Letters of Sherwood Anderson*; George Woodberry from the *Selected Letters of George Woodberry*.